Polar Bears and Penguins

A Compare and Contrast Book

by Katharine Hall

Polar bears live in the Arctic, in
the Northern Hemisphere . . .

. . . but penguins live in
the Southern Hemisphere.

Some penguins live in the water around Antarctica. They come onto land to lay eggs and raise their young.

The Arctic is an ocean surrounded by continents. Sea ice floats on the water.

Antarctica is a continent surrounded by oceans. Ice and snow cover the land.

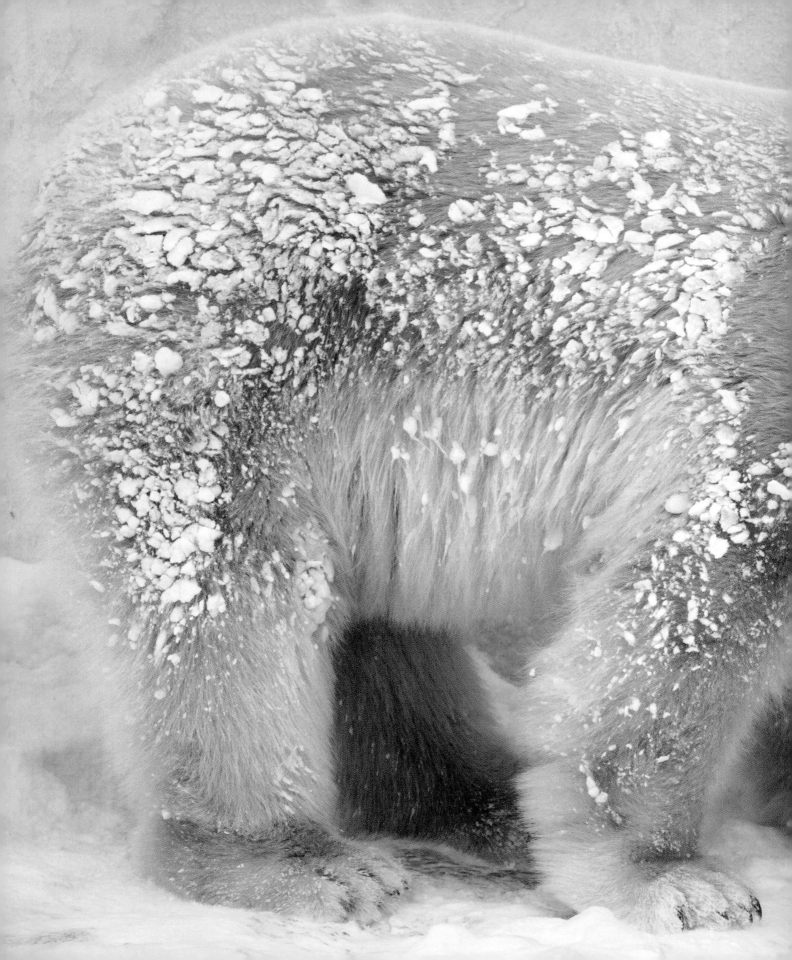

Polar bears are covered in fur.

Penguins are covered in feathers.

A polar bear is a type of bear.

black bear

giant panda bear

grizzly bear

sloth bear

sun bear

polar bear

There are many different types of penguins.

African penguin

emperor penguin

Adelie penguin

rockhopper penguin

little penguin

yellow-eyed penguin

Polar bears roam alone or in small groups of a mother and her young cubs.

Penguins gather in giant colonies that can number in the hundreds or thousands.

Up in the Arctic,
December occurs during
winter and in darkness.

Down in the Antarctic, December occurs during summer and in sunshine.

Polar bears and penguins live at opposite ends of the Earth.

For Creative Minds

Seasons

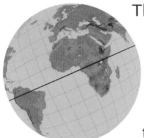

The **Equator** is an imaginary line that divides the Earth into two halves or **hemispheres**. Everything north of the Equator is in the Northern Hemisphere. Everything south of the Equator is in the Southern Hemisphere.

The Earth rotates on an axis that has a 23.4° tilt. This causes the seasons. When one hemisphere is tilted toward the Sun, it has longer days and more sunlight. At the same time, the other hemisphere has shorter days and less sunlight. The season in the northern half of the world is always the opposite of the season in the southern half.

Polar Mammals

Mammals live in both the Arctic and the Antarctic. All mammals have backbones, breathe air, are warm-blooded, and grow hair on their bodies. Young mammals drink milk from their mothers after they are born. There are only a few mammals native to Antarctica and they are all marine mammals (they spend most of their lives in the water). The Arctic is home to both land mammals and marine mammals.

Seals are marine mammals that live in both the Arctic and the Antarctic. Down in the Antarctic, leopard seals hunt penguins. Up in the Arctic, polar bears hunt ringed seals.

Humans are a type of mammal. Many people live in the Arctic.

Only a few researchers and scientists live in Antarctica.

A Year at the Poles

During the winter, male Emperor Penguins hold eggs on top of their feet and cover them with a fold of skin to keep them safe and warm until they hatch.

In the spring, the chicks are old enough that they can be left in crèches while both parents hunt for food. Some crèches hold thousands of young chicks guarded by adult penguins.

Before long, the chicks are old enough to travel to the sea. They spend the warm summer months learning to hunt and avoid predatory seals.

In late autumn, Emperor penguins gather into giant colonies to breed. They travel to nesting sites 30 to 75 miles (50-120 kilometers) inland.

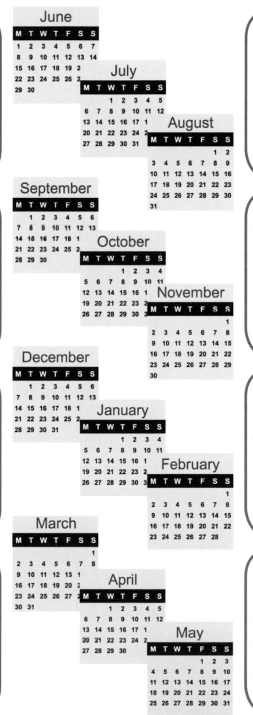

Food is hard to come by in summers, when the sea ice is far from land. Many polar bears swim toward land to hunt smaller prey on land and in the water as they wait for the sea ice to return.

As temperatures drop in the late fall, pregnant polar bears make their dens in the snow. Other adult polar bears venture out onto the sea ice to hunt for seals.

Mother polar bears give birth in the dens where they will spend their winter. There are usually two cubs in each litter. Mother and cubs stay in the warm den until the cubs can face the cold air outside.

In the spring, when the cubs are a few months old, they leave the den. Cubs grow strong drinking their mother's milk and eating the seals she catches.

Polar Bear True or False

1. Polar bears live on every continent.
2. The Arctic is named for its polar bears.
3. Polar bears have fur on the bottom of their feet.
4. An adult polar bear can stand 8 feet (2.4 meters) tall.
5. Polar bears have white skin under their fur.
6. There are more polar bears in the world than there are people.
7. Polar bears are long-distance swimmers.
8. Polar bears are the only bears in the Arctic.
9. Polar bears only eat seals.
10. The only predators polar bears have are humans.

Answers: 1-False. Polar bears live in the arctic regions of North America, Europe, and Asia. 2-True. "Arctic" comes from the Greek word for bear, "arktos." Antarctica means "without bears." 3-True. The hair on their feet helps them stay warm and not slip on the ice. 4-True. 5-False. Underneath their fur, polar bears have black skin that helps to better trap the Sun's heat. 6-False. Polar bears are an endangered species and there are only 20,000 to 25,000 polar bears in the world. 7-True. Although most tracked swims are closer to 96 miles (155km), the longest swim that researchers have tracked is 220 miles (354km). 8-False. Brown bears' territory overlaps with polar bears' in some areas. 9-False. Ringed seals are polar bears' favorite prey, but in the summer when the ice is thawed, bears will hunt muskox, reindeer, birds, rodents, crustaceans, and other small prey. 10-True.

Penguin Matching

All wild penguins live in the Southern Hemisphere. Penguins live in many different places, not just in Antarctica. Penguins spend most of their lives in the water, but come up on land or ice to mate and nest. Can you match the descriptions of the penguins below with their location on the map?

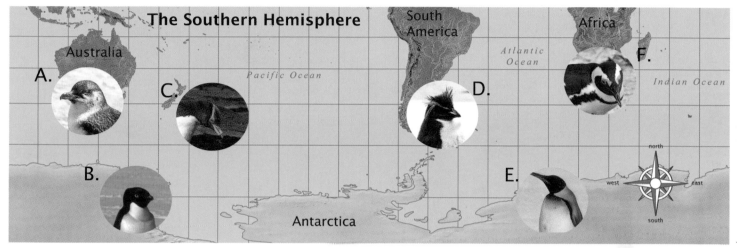

1. Unlike most penguins, rockhopper penguins don't waddle. Instead, they hop and bound from rock to rock. The largest rockhopper colonies are found in the Falkland Islands off South America. Rockhoppers have spiky yellow and black crests on their heads.

2. Yellow-eyed penguins are native to New Zealand, an island country in the Pacific Ocean, to the east of Australia. They have yellow eyes, a yellow band of feathers around the back of their head, and pink feet. Yellow-eyed penguins are endangered and there are less than 4,000 of them in the world.

3. The little penguin is the smallest of all penguin species and stands 13 inches (33cm) tall. Little penguins have blue feathers on their wings and backs. They are also called fairy penguins or little blue penguins. Most little penguin colonies are in Australia and the little penguins return to the same site every year to breed.

4. Adelie penguins live in and around Antarctica. They are excellent swimmers and can dive as deep as 575 feet (175 meters). Adelie penguins line their nests with stones and small pebbles. Sometimes adults steal pebbles from other penguins' nests.

5. The African penguin is also called the black-footed penguin. African penguins are endangered and live along the coasts of southern Africa. They have black spots on their chest and each penguin's spots are unique, just like a human's fingerprints!

6. Emperor penguins are black and white with yellow feathers on the upper chest and around the ears. They are the tallest and heaviest of all penguins, standing 48 to 51 inches (110 to 130cm) high. Emperor penguins live in and around Antarctica.

To my niblings, Kevin and Amiya—KH

Thanks to Dr. Carol Landis, co-Principal Investigator on the *Beyond Penguins and Polar Bears* project, for reviewing the accuracy of the information in this book.

Library of Congress Cataloging-in-Publication Data

Hall, Katharine, 1989- author.
 Polar bears and penguins : a compare and contrast book / by Katharine Hall.
     pages cm. -- (Compare and contrast books)
   Audience: 4-8.
 ISBN 978-1-62855-209-6 (English hardcover) -- ISBN 978-1-62855-218-8 (English pbk.)
-- ISBN 978-1-62855-236-2 (English ebook downloadable) -- ISBN 978-1-62855-254-6
(English ebook dual language enhanced) -- ISBN 978-1-62855-227-0 (Spanish pbk.)
-- ISBN 978-1-62855-245-4 (Spanish ebook downloadable) -- ISBN 978-1-62855-263-8
(Spanish ebook dual language enhanced)
1. Polar bear--Juvenile literature. 2. Penguins--Juvenile literature. 3. Animals--Polar
regions--Juvenile literature. 4. Adaptation (Biology)--Juvenile literature. I. Title.
 QL737.C27H3585 2014
 591.70911--dc23
                              2013044813

Photo Credits:

Photo content	*Source or Photographer*
polar bear-north	Elena Shchipkova, Shutterstock
penguins-south	Volodymyr Goinyk, Shutterstock
polar bear-Arctic Ocean	Yvonne Pijnenburg-Schonewille, Shutterstock
penguins-Antarctica	Volodymyr Goinyk, Shutterstock
polar bear-fur	Zhiltsov Alexandr, Shutterstock
penguin-feathers	Andrew Bignell, Shutterstock
black bear	Mike Bender, USFWS, public domain
giant panda bear	Ronald Carlson, public domain
sloth bear	Rob Francis, Shutterstock
grizzly bear	Adam Van Spronsen, Shutterstock
sun bear	Benzine, Shutterstock
polar bear cub on mother	U.S. Fish and Wildlife, public domain
African penguin	Niall Dunne, Shutterstock
emperor penguin	William Ju, Shutterstock
Adelie penguins	John Bortniak, NOAA, public domain
rockhopper penguin	Dean Bertoncelj, Shutterstock
little penguin	Khoroshunova Olga, Shutterstock
yellow-eyed pentuiin	Nickolay Stanev, Shutterstock
polar bear-family	Outdoorsman, Shutterstock
penguin-colony	Watchtheworld, Shutterstock
polar bear-December	Kotomiti Okuma, Shutterstock
penguins-December	Willem Tims, Shutterstock
polar bear-jumping	Don Landwehrle, Shutterstock
penguins-jumping	Anton Ivanov, Shutterstock
Arctic village (FCM)	Mark Serreze, NSIDC, public domain
leopard seal (FCM)	Peter Griffin, public domain
ringed seal (FCM)	Lee Cooper, NSF, public domain
Adelie penguin (FCM)	Michael Van Woert, NOAA, public domain

key phrases for educators: adaptations, climate, compare/contrast, geography, habitat, life science

Available in Spanish as ***Osos Polares y Pingüinos: Un libro de comparación y contraste***

Manufactured in China, January 2015
This product conforms to CPSIA 2008
Second Printing

Arbordale Publishing
formerly Sylvan Dell Publishing
Mt. Pleasant, SC 29464
www.ArbordalePublishing.com